APPALACHIA: A SELF-PORTRAIT

PHOTOGRAPHS BY

LYN ADAMS

SHELBY ADAMS

ROBERT COOPER

EARL DOTTER

WILL ENDRES

WENDY EWALD

LINDA MANSBERGER

APPALACHIA: A SELF-PORTRAIT

Edited by

WENDY EWALD

Foreword by ROBERT COLES

Text by LOYAL JONES

GNOMON PRESS for Appalshop, Inc.

Front cover photograph of Rena Cornett was taken by
Wendy Ewald in Letcher County, Kentucky; back cover
photograph of Lockard Farm was taken by Robert Cooper
between Cox's Mill & Glenville, West Virginia; frontispiece
photograph of a homestead in Hardy County, West Virginia,
was taken by Earl Dotter.

ISBN 0–917788–20–6

Library of Congress Catalogue Card Number 79–52385

The publication of this book is supported by a grant
from the National Endowment for the Arts, a Federal Agency.

This book is published by Gnomon Press, P.O. Box 106,
Frankfort, Kentucky 40602 for Appalshop, a non-profit
media collective located in Whitesburg, Kentucky.

Typeset in Sabon by Graphic Composition, Inc.

Printed by Rapoport Printing Company using
their Stonetone process.

FOREWORD

Robert Coles

In a letter to a friend, written in 1950, William Carlos Williams commented on his work as a physician and a poet: "I try to take care of the sick, the needy; but I keep my eye on them, because down and out as they are in Paterson, New Jersey, they have a lot to teach me. Sometimes I'll be driving home, and I'll see the people I've met that day in my mind's eye, as clear as can be. When I write my poems, I'll try to hand over what I've seen to others, through words. If I were a photographer, I'd send out pictures!"

His poems were vivid, compelling—faithful, always, to the truth of lives witnessed carefully, sensitively. He was an intermediary of sorts, anxious to convey to others what he himself saw everyday; and anxious to acknowledge in the people he knew the dignity and resourcefulness and courage which he knew attend their various actions. These photographs and accompanying personal statements (declarations of intent, descriptions, modest but forthright, of work undertaken and successfully accomplished) belong to a documentary tradition Dr. Williams valued highly and contributed to as a writer. It is not presumptious, I believe, to make mention of him here, or of the well known collaboration between James Agee and Walker Evans. These earnest and perceptive Appalachian photographers want to struggle for a kind of visual truth that reaches out and touches the viewer—reminds him or her that others, different in many ways, are fellow human beings, struggling as all of us do with life's uncertainties, complexities, assorted hurdles and fateful circumstances.

It is unnecessary and arrogant indeed for an outsider, no matter the years he has spent in West Virginia and Eastern Kentucky, to put any seal of approval on what this cooperative venture has to offer. Nor is an *explication de texte* in the least desirable. These talented and decent photographers (utterly without the curse of self-centeredness, a hazard for all of us who write or take pictures, day in day out) have been at pain to respond with attentive affection and continuing concern to the proud people of a much misrepresented and historically significant part of the American Scene. The result is a social and cultural education for all of us—with no fallout of condescension or smugness. The result, too is a gift—the recognition successful art gives us of ourselves, reflected (in this case) through the glimpses of others caught by a number of cameras.

A REMEMBRANCE

Loyal Jones

This place and people: Appalachia, Southern Highlands, Southern Mountains, Appalachians, Highlanders, Southern Mountaineers, hillbillies, briarhoppers. John Campbell wrote that more is known that isn't so about this place and people than any other on the globe. Perhaps so. The old stereotypes and supposed facts are pervasive. Almost everyone has an opinion of this place, whether or not he has any firsthand knowledge. How does one describe this place and people? It depends on who is doing the looking and his assumptions, attitudes and cultural baggage. It depends on the relationship between the looker and the looked-at, the photographer and the photographed, the recorder and the recorded. In the end we who are part of the region and who try to describe it can only report what we have seen, what has happened to us and what we have come to believe. When we compare our pictures, we know that the same land and people are different to each of us. So it is everywhere.

Appalachia has changed, some would say for the better, some for worse. Many of the people have become, on the surface at least, much like their countrymen elsewhere, but there are others who have held on to the old ways with stubborn vim. Time and progress and a host of fads have eroded away parts of the traditional life of the mountains, and new traditions are being formed. Yet, much that I observed and was a part of as a boy is still with us. Considering the changes that have transformed much of this country and the world in the past fifty years, that is a remarkable fact.

We who were born into Appalachia and the Depression at the same time were the lucky ones. Our people, most of them, had been in training a long time for the challenge of living without money. My family had a team of horses, implements, a brood sow, prolific Rhode Island Reds, seed corn and beans and plenty of land, even if the price for using it was a rent of half the crop. We always ate but listened to our parents, Democrats, grumble at the only one they knew to grumble at, Hoover.

We fared better than most, although many of the jokes were about hard times and food. Daddy told about visiting people who had only sorghum and cornbread for dinner, but the host graciously commanded him to "reach and get anything you want." Another story was about a woman going to the governor of the state to plead for him to let her husband out of the penitentiary.

"What's he in for?" asked the governor.

"For stealing a ham," she replied.

"Is he a good man?"

"Well, no. He's rough on me and the kids."

"He's a good worker, though, isn't he?"

"Well, actually he won't hardly work at all."

"Then why would you want a man like this out of the penitentiary?"

"Governor, we're out of ham."

Our next-door neighbor, out of work and no farmer, found a way to hold off starvation. "Found" isn't the right word; he implemented what he already knew. He built a still for the top of their kitchen stove, thus fooling any roving revenuers looking for suspicious smoke. But he had a problem with friendly neighbor children. His vigilant wife headed me off at the front door and kept me on the front porch during my visits. She once gave me a ceramic model of Noah's Ark to keep me distracted. I have it still, a reminder of two long-gone kindly people who coped the best they could in difficult times.

My mother and father, who were strong Missionary Baptists, withheld judgment but strongly disapproved of such coping, however. While they did not until many years later tell me how our neighbors kept body and soul together, they warned me against the evils of strong drink. And well my father should, since he had tasted the bitter dregs of sin. In what has been called, rightly or wrongly, the pattern of the mountains, Daddy helled around a bit in his early married days, while Mama, a preacher's daughter faithful to the Baptist church, prayed for him. His day of reckoning came one dark night when he attempted to find his way home with an internal load of someone's moonshine and wandered into a laurel hell, aptly named. He thrashed around and sought escape through the long night while he both sobered and froze. By dawn, he had turned to the Lord, and he never retreated, never touched liquor again, except as cough medicine, properly mixed with honey. Therefore, he spoke with authority on the subject of liquor. This talk had a profound effect on me. One day I was slipping through the woods near our house when I saw a well-known bootlegger and his henchmen unloading suitcases and trunks into an abandoned chicken house. When they left I examined their cargo and found it to be fruit jars of moonshine whiskey. Fancying myself to be a junior soldier of the Lord, I ran home to get a box of Epsom Salts to doctor the cache, imagining, no doubt, that I would thus teach a lesson to the man's customers. My mother caught me on the way out and asked for an explanation. She was impressed with my zeal but concerned for my future health, since the bootlegger was known as a dangerous character. I can see him still, dark features under a black felt hat, clad in white shirt and blue serge suit and black kangaroo shoes, sinister, like the right-hand man to Old Scratch himself. While I was bogged down in the conflict between zeal and cowardice, the mover of spirits returned with a new pair of conspiritors and a different vehicle with blocked-up springs in the rear so as to fool the sheriff, and they loaded up the whiskey and departed, while I watched from behind a sourwood bush. In those days there were no phones around, and the sheriff was fifteen miles away in the county seat. We probably would not have notified him anyway, even if it were easy to do so. We believed in killing our own snakes, so to speak, even if we let a few get away.

Most of the people I knew in those days were honest hard-working folks, who did the best they could with what they had. This was all that their religious beliefs required of them. Most were Baptists with a strong dose of Calvinism, especially in regard to the human condition. They looked upon life as tragic, not just because they were poor and suffered a lot, but because they perceived so well what they ought to and ought not to do, and failed fairly regularly in achieving the ideal. Of course, there were some Methodists and Pentecostals around who had a sterner view of things, being perfectionists. They honestly believed that one could be lifted above sin. They knew, though it was always nip and tuck, and therefore they tried to get rid of any tempta-

tions that might rear and flaunt among the faithful. They had a disastrous effect on dancing, fiddling and banjo picking. Some would rail against painted lips, displayed legs or other distracting practices. We Baptists would sometimes scoff indulgently at such a notion that a bundle of flesh could rise above temptations. But the perfectionists eventually had their effect on the whole society, and Baptists began to preach sermons that greatly modified the traditional Calvinism, to the effect that some of the most satisfying worldly pleasures such as picking and singing were put on the blacklist.

My worst times were when the annual revival meeting conflicted with the folk dancing at the local settlement school. Since my father was a deacon and my mother a pillar of the church, much was expected of me. People noticed when I was not at a church meeting, and anyway, though I was unenthusiastic in the job, I was often called on to lead the singing. Folk dancing, always diplomatically called "folk games," was considered to be all right by most of the Baptist people, unlike the frowned-upon square dances that were held here and there, but this assumed that church work took precedence over everything else. I had to resort to some ruses in order to get to at least some of the dancing. Fortunately, everything is informal, in the usual sense, in a country church. People come and go during the long revival nights, either answering the call of nature, the urge to smoke or to exhort among the sinner friends. Therefore, I could saunter out after a reasonable stay, then break into a mad dash through the woods to the nearby school for a few turns with the outlander girls who were not bound by our local traditions.

While I had the boldness to slip out and go dancing, I did not have the independence of mind to enjoy it, like one fellow I knew said, "You know the Baptists and the Methodists are not that different; they both sin, but the Methodists just can't enjoy it." I can see now that the hardest taskmaster of all is one's own conscience, and I know now too that that little Baptist church, heavily influenced by the perfectionism that was spreading through the land, laid a sensitive conscience on those of us who took it seriously.

That church, and others like it, gave us a sense of home and place. A hymn goes:

> Coming home, coming home,
> Never more to roam.
> Open wide thine arms of love,
> Lord, I'm coming home.

Coming back to one's native place, and turning back to God are two desires that are related in the hearts of Appalachian wanderers. Kin, neighbors, the land, the church are intertwined in memory—the locusts of summer, the remembered voices of esteemed relatives and friends, the persuasive revival hymns on sweltering nights, the cadenced sermons, the pastel glow of homeland hills beckons in the night, wherever we are. I see the funeral processions with license plates from Ohio, Indiana, Michigan, bringing another one home. The young miner felled by the slate, who has stayed near home but has wandered away from the faith of his fathers, goes to rest with the Old Regular Baptists. Most of those who grew up in one of the strong mountain churches and have drifted away from its teachings will also eventually return to some degree of faith if they live long enough. Most who move physically away from their place on earth will also want to return. Many never leave except to get enough money to do what they want to back home, like my neighbor who toiled in the Akron rubber factories to get enough money to buy the farm which his wife and sons were tilling all the while. It is well-known that the north-south roads in and out of the mountains are clogged on Friday and Sunday evenings. There are stories about this homing instinct, like the one about a man who died and went to heaven, met St. Peter, toured the streets of gold, listened appreciatively to the harps and the choirs, but was jarred by a wailing off in a far corner of Heaven where he saw people chained to a wall.

"Who are those people?" he inquired of St. Peter.

"Appalachian mountaineers."

"Why are they in chains?"

"To keep them from going home every week-end."

Margaret Mead commented once that Appalachian people migrate to cities up North, but that they leave their souls back down in Tennessee or Kentucky. For one thing, their people are buried back home. Nothing ties one to a place like having forebears and relatives resting in little hillside cemeteries.

Two years ago I visited the two graveyards where most of my departed people lie.

Blessed are those who have not seen and yet have believed.

My parents would have liked that epitaph, because they lived by faith and expected grace. They lie on the brow of a little hill, to which my father once pointed as a good place to be, facing the rising sun in the mountain burial tradition. When I pondered on their legacy to me, I regretted the time when I was ashamed of who we were, of being poor, of being common people. I could not remember when they did not try to do the right thing by us children, by neighbors, even by strangers. My father had a hard time of doing right, since he struggled, as do I, with a virulent temper. My father was gentle, but gruff and took his role as a deacon in the Baptist Church seriously. He had, too, the stubbornness that seems to run through all of my people. His mettle was constantly being tested by the kind of horses he kept as work animals. They were as independent and vexatious as the rest of us probably were. Princess, a Section 8 Cavalry reject complete with US brand, was a dream of a plow-horse but was unpredictable as a mount, sometimes going docilely along and then exploding into wild fence-rowing, sunfishing gyrations, throwing everyone sky-high who tried her. Lucy threw fits at inopportune moments. My most

exciting times were when my father became exasperated with their shenani-gans and lashed them into a dead run across the fields ahead of a careening wagon until the devilment in them was subdued. I think Princess and Lucy enjoyed those runs as much as my father and I did. He loved that unlikely pair of bays and kept them fat as butterballs.

My mother was a gentle soul who let us know exactly what was expected of us. She worked from dawn to late at night, as hard as any woman ever worked, cleaning, cooking, gardening, milking, canning, quilting, mending. She never indicated that her role was a secondary one and never questioned her purpose in life. She took the lead in matters having to do with education, health and religion. She instituted the nightly Bible reading and prayer and grace at meals. What she expected of us children, for the most part, she got.

I know now the value of their companionship and example. They taught me the truths I have encountered among other mountain people: that everyone is intrinsically as good as anyone else but no better; that a person, not his ancestors, is responsible for who he is and what he does; that everybody does about the best he can with what he has, and that it is usually futile to pass rigid judgments on others' actions because you never know what special burdens they carry around which may limit thought and hamper actions. Shadows of Calvinism.

My grandparents on both sides lie in the other Baptist church graveyard. As I grew up, theirs and other familiar names on the gravestones populated the conversations around the dinner table. I am kin to half the names—Jones, Morgan, May, Beatty. My grandpa on the Jones side never wanted to be buried in this cemetery, because he had been turned out of that very church over an altercation with my uncle, his son-in-law, over politics, or so it was told to me. Grandma was already buried there, and most of his people, and so his children did what they had to do—put him where he had to be even against his will. My memories of Grandpa are clearer than my recollection of Grandma, who died earlier. Grandpa came to live with us after Grandma died. He, who had been a storekeeper, farmer and a prankster, was solemn behind his white beard when he lived with us, unhappy without Grandma, his store and farm. He soon returned to the place of his memories, under the watchful eyes of my aunt who lived nearby. Sitting in the graveyard, I remembered my visits with my grandparents and playing with the Shields boys who lived across the fields and who were specialists in making truck wagons—daredevil conveyances with blackgum wheels and wooden chassis, which you guided down the precipitous slopes with your feet on the front axles. Grandma Jones was probably in constant dread that I would go home maimed for life.

Grandpa Morgan went to glory in the middle of an energetic sermon with the same text and in the same Baptist pulpit where he preached his ordination sermon forty-nine years earlier. His death came the year before I was born, but I grew up hearing about him. He was named Francis Marion Morgan, for the Revolutionary general, although he went by the initials of F.M. He was known as a great preacher. I know of his long trips through the mountains to serve remote churches on the back of Selum, the heroic family horse. As a boy I was fascinated by the strand of Selum's mane that was tacked to the back porch wall. Grandpa's saddlebags, stuffed with letters from those who were related to his church work as well as flyers from religious publishing houses, were passed on to me along with one of his Bibles containing sermon notes. They help to illumine his life and work.

Grandma Morgan lived nearly thirty years beyond her husband. She was a

Earl Dotter

feisty and witty old lady, set in her ways, quite confident that her thinking and doing were logical and universal. She sat in the same chair, ate from the same plate and used the same utensils as long as I knew her, and no one dared to touch what was so personally hers. Her straight-back chair had legs four inches shorter than the others from its being hitched forward and backward on the fireplace hearth over her lifetime. She had a special chair for her favorite cat, and everyone avoided that chair too. She lived life on her own terms, for the most part, and people for miles around spoke of her independence. I spent a week or two with her each summer of my childhood, and I remember clearest the supper meals, always with huge boiled potatoes and fresh butter, ham or homemade sausage and plenty of creamy milk. I also was fascinated by the ever-running spigot on the back porch, bringing water from a high bold spring on the mountain in back of her house. It poured into a trough where the milk and butter were kept. Two years back, when I visited the graveyards, I went by the old house again. The roof was falling in and the doors sagging, but the spigot on the decaying back proch was running boldly through a bottomless trough, a strong reminder of another day, another way of life that lingers in my memory and attitudes.

During that visit, I also went about the community in which my mother and father were born and raised, to talk with people, in an attempt to get an idea of how much Appalachian people and values have changed from their time to mine. Two interviews stand out. The first was with an 83-year-old man to whose house I wandered, looking for my uncle Weimer Cochran (with whom I had the second talk). He came to his front door with pistol on hip, cordial but aloof until I mentioned that I was Alex Jones' boy, whereupon I was greeted as warmly as a relative. He hung the pistol up as a sign of hospitality and spoke affectionately of my family, with the exception of one with whom he had trouble as a young man. He described my kinsman as an overbearing person who had promised to whip him. He related the following incident to me:

> I met him down here one day. We'd had a little jower, and he said he was a goin' to lick me. I stuck my gun down in my front pocket. I walked down the road next to that high bank. He was over on the other side. When he got about thirty feet from me, I seen a different look on his face, and he hollered at me, 'Hey, let's make friends.' I said, 'If that suits you it does me.' He walked up, and we shook hands. Just at the drop of a hat, if he'd just made a little move, I'd a shot him full of holes. That's what was in my mind. I wouldn't want to hurt nobody, but now, that's just how close I come to gettin' in bad trouble. Oh, I knowed he was a way bigger than I was. He could a whipped me in a fair fight.

He said one other thing that stuck in my mind:

> I know more Bible right today than half the preachers tryin' to preach. I've read it a whole lot. I can keep up with any preacher that gets up there. I can keep right on his trail.

There is a clue to mountain violence. It is usually not perpetrated by lawless uncaring persons, but by ordinarily decent ones whose pride and honor are at stake. There too are the seeds of mountain independence and self-reliance—pride and competence in physical matters and knowledge and self-assurance in the realm of spirit and thought.

Weimer Cochran was a quintessential mountain man, who was proud of his Scottish ancestry, proud of his two hundred acres of steep mountain land on which he had made a tolerable living raising magnificent potatoes for the restaurants and hotels in the area before they switched to frozen french fries. He was married to my mother's sister, who had birthed two sons, one of whom was lost in World War II. Uncle Weimer had been a rough and ready scrapper in his prime, having once broken my Uncle Cliff's jaw when both were drinking together, putting Cliff on soup for a month. Now, at 84, he was mellow and reflective and unwilling to talk of that side of his nature. He had attended a one-room school and since then had read everything he could get his hands on that enlightened him on matters of interest. He spoke of the Revolution as if it were World War II. He knew what it was all about.

> I've read about Scotland and England, about the pestilence and all of them old feuds. They had no law, not up until the sixteenth and seventeenth century. They had no stable laws. The United States had the first stable laws, you know that? Now England and some of them countries were making a stagger at it. But when America got her independence, she led the world in establishing the rights of man. There's no question about that, but it took a long time to do that. When we got our independence, we were under the rule of tyrants right on. That old Federalist Party was just controlled by the rich. You couldn't vote if you didn't have land. It was controlled by the rich. But these fellers that helped win that Revolutionary War, you see, they took their pay in land. They went on west, settled down. They were voters. They voted Thomas Jefferson in power. Thomas, he was a great man, I believe the greatest that America produced at that time, I'm honest about it. He believed in the rights of the little feller. "Give him dignity! He's not a man without dignity. Give him his right to vote, even if he ain't got property. When you give a man the right to vote, you give him his dignity!" Now, that was Tom's theory, and he was right about it. It proved out that way. Why Daniel Webster said on the floor of the Senate, "If you give the common man the right to vote we'll be in anarchy." Yeah! A United States Senator! He just didn't have the faith in man that he oughta had.
>
> The Declaration of Independence was the greatest article that was ever drawn, I honestly believe it. It was a good idea that Thomas Jefferson drew that up because no other man, before or since, has had the sense to draw up an article like that. There was a man, boys, that had something. He was a great man.

And on other subjects:

> The old ways are fading out. There is a saying that the best for today will not be best for tomorrow. The new gradually takes over. You won't notice it, but the new will replace the old. Oftentimes it is a mistake. I'm old-fashioned.
>
> I'll tell you two of the greatest secrets of life. The first secret for man or woman, boy or girl, for success, is self-dominion. Learn to control yourself. That is the greatest thing a human can attain. And the next one is learn to do without. If you don't have the best, use the next-best.

There was more, but this gives a flavor of the thought and convictions of one mountain man. He died this year, and I know that there are no more just like him, and yet, for me, he represented so much of what I have observed in other mountain people. He had his faults and knew it, but he had ideals and was master of his situation.

The cemeteries, the people with whom I talked, the magnificent land, had a great and lasting effect on me. We are bound together.

Uncle Weimer was unusual in that he tried to figure out where his people, his wife's and my people came from and how they might have fit into the beginning of this country. Most of my people are vague about their origins, except for the family names which they can reel off. When asked where our people came from originally, they name the Yadkin country, that name having stuck in someone's memory. Not knowing is a kind of modesty and humility, of not putting too much emphasis on self. They would, for the most part, be uncomfortable with the Sons and Daughters of the Revolution, who try to trace their ancestors. I well remember one relative claiming to have traced our people back to John Paul Jones. This news met with some derision or at least indulgent smiles, especially after I or someone came home from school with the information that the old admiral was a bachelor. The only ancestors who were important were those one could remember or whose graves you could visit on Decoration Day. They vaguely knew that most of our people had come from the British Isles and made much of the fact that Grandma Morgan, a Weatherman before she married, was Dutch. They attributed her independent and sassy ways to that fact. They might also talk of someone's being Irish or German or Scottish. They were interested in personality, sometimes speculating on what gave a certain person his special characteristics. For example, if he were florid and possessed of a temper, it might be said that this was the Irish (probably Scotch-Irish) in him. For the most part, though, the leveling ideals dominated, and people did not know much, and therefore did not talk much, about their forebears, except for the ones they had known. It was the people in the county seats, or on the valley farms, orthe smartened-up mountaineers who spent their time poring over genealogy lists. Most people felt that they were stuck with the genes they had and that finding out about illustrious ancestors would not improve them one whit. Anyhow, they knew that one was as likely to find a horse thief or moonshiner as he was to find a person of noble distinction.

The notion that many people have about mountain isolation is not wholly accurate. My people came from a section of a county in North Carolina that was settled after the Civil War, partly by soldiers from both sides. I grew up hearing tales of the war and about Union and Confederate veterans who had seen a great deal of the country. The Spanish-American War and World War I took many people from all parts of the mountains to foreign places. My Uncle Cliff Morgan was in France in the latter war. My Uncle Will Jones was a career man in the Navy. Two of my uncles went West for a time, one visiting all of the western states, according to him, except Nevada and Utah. Many people from my area went to Oregon and Washington to work in the timber industry there, after most of the virgin timber had been cut from Appalachia. Two of my cousins came from North Carolina to Kentucky to work in the coal mines. Several of my cousins went to Georgia, Ohio, Michigan and other places to work in factories. They tended to come and go, living in the mountains part of the year or when there were jobs and going elsewhere when there was no way of making it at home. My brothers and sisters and I live in North Carolina (east and west), Kentucky, Arizona and Delaware. Military and maritime service during and after World War II took four of us to many parts of the world.

The differences that many say they observe in mountain people are not primarily a result of isolation, even though it may appear to a stranger to be so. The fact that so many mountain people return home from farflung places to take up mountain lifestyles again indicates that mountaineer differences lie imbedded as much in values as in place.

With the publication of Henry Shapiro's *Appalachia on Our Mind* (University of North Carolina Press, 1978) the question of Appalachian differences has become an issue again. The writers and the scholars opined for years on the subject while mountaineers went on doing what they do, saying what they say and believing what they do, puzzled at the attention, angered at spurious opinions, their feelings tinged with both pride and shame over it all. The writers, such as Mary Noailles Murfree and John Fox, Jr., made a few dollars in the process of stereotyping mountain people through their emphasis on the quaint (ballads and dress and speech) and the chillingly alluring (feuding and moonshining). Other writers have touched on the bizarre (religious practices, folk medicine and faith healing). With the "uplift" era came stories of the

Earl Dotter / Dry Branch Coal Camp

appalling ignorance of the people. With the War on Poverty and related on-slaughts came imposition of the Culture of overty theory of people on a cir-cular sorghum mill trip constantly being reinforced and weighted down by the shortcomings of their sub-culture. Later still the radical onslaught brought a new theory that viewed us mountain people as victims of all sorts of foreign exploiters. Still others, the developers, have seen us as merely underdeveloped. All of these pictures that have been widely disseminated, hatched a multitude of programs to cure whatever the perceived ailment was. And thousands of workers have descended on us, each with a hundred notions about us that had been instilled by theorists long before they had ever seen one of us.

The country as a whole has changed more than the mountains, making it appear that somehow the mountain people became different. Some have called this the lingering frontier. Perhaps, but the same people who exhibit old-fash-ioned beliefs may also be modern in other ways. For example, they may grow huge gardens, planted on the right time of the moon but store the fruits thereof in General Electric freezers.

The religion of mountain people has common elements with the belief of ordinary people throughout the country. The basic element is fundamentalism (a word that has been put out of favor by the liberal Christians), an attempt to get down to the nub of what it's all about. My opinion is that much of mountain character and values grows out of the old Calvinism, mainly that of Old School Baptists. They viewed life as tragic, man as fragile and fallible, God as all-knowing and religion as forming a relationship with God who will save believers through grace, a reward for belief and not works. The favorite scriptures, mainly from St. Paul, stress tolerance and forebearance, doing the best you can (which usually isn't anything to brag about), traditional ways in regard to worship, family and personal relationships. True, the perfectionists, such as Methodists and Pentecostals, have modified Calvinism and taught a belief in human perfection, but the old perception of man clings on in the face of forceful and optimistic sermons. The main thrust of the Pentecostal movement grew out of the Appalachian mountains, fueled, no doubt, by a deep longing for evidence of hope in regard to the earthly human state. It stressed a means of proving that one was a conduit for the Holy Spirit. At first it was the speaking in tongues and shouting. Later a very few went further to take up serpents, to drink poison and to test the flames. Many outsiders have thought of all Appalachians as being either snake handlers or hardshell Baptists. It is a confusing picture to the uninformed, to be sure. We in the mountains are as varied in our denominational beliefs as groups elsewhere, but our religion has a rural flavor and a lingering stamp of Calvinism. These beliefs have been a factor in shaping the old-fashioned, independent nature of the people, who feel obligated to resist the change that is recommended by the optimistic doers of good who perennially stalk the mountains.

Perhaps, as Dr. Shapiro implies, there is no Appalachia, that it is a creation of the minds of writers, perpetuated by all of us for our own purposes. But if so, why is it that both mountaineer and mainline American go away shaking their heads after an encounter, don't feel at home with one another, don't appear to understand each other, don't seem to want the same things out of life, resist one another out of misunderstanding, fear or skepticism? When the mountaineer moves to the city, he speaks of the strange ways of city people. Likewise, the community helpers of the city—the police, teachers, health authorities, ministers and welfare workers—speak of the mountaineer's strange ways. They may try to shame him, his wife, and children into becoming good unobtrusive city folk. Often, it seems to me, the mountaineer doesn't really care what the city folk think, except that he deeply resents being looked down on. Many hate the city and endure it only because they have to. I remember stopping for gas in Columbus, Ohio, once. The man pumping gas saw my Kentucky plates and began to talk about Kentucky. I found that he was from Barbourville. "Do you like Columbus?" I inquired, and before I was through the second syllable of the last word, he answered with great feeling, "Hell no!" He had gone there because there was no work in Barbourville, and he stayed now because all of his relatives and friends were dead or gone from his old home. He was not a happy man. Home to him, to all of us, is a feeling. Columbus did not feel like home to him. In one's home place, if it is a rural personal place, one feels as much as he hears or sees. The way people look at you or otherwise act, their choice of words and their inflections are often more important than what they actually say. There are many nuances of meaning in all human interaction. When one is in a strange culture, he may feel out of place, even if he is communicating at a certain level with others. Appalachian culture is a set of feelings about people, life and things. Those without those feelings may feel strange here. Likewise, those of us who grew up here, when we go elsewhere, even though we may have gained a worldly sophistication, we do not feel entirely at home.

All of this does not prove an Appalachian culture. It only proves, to me at least, that there is such a reality as culture and that there are infinite cultural variations as one may travel from one part of this country to another, and these variations do affect people in profound ways.

The Appalachia I have seen is a land of contrasts—coal mines and valley farms, strip mines and verdant forests, crystal springs and polluted rivers, folk medicine and computer science, ballads and rock and roll, people of immense wealth and paupers, people of iron character and vote-sellers, Ph.D.'s and illiterates, high churchmen and snake handlers. These contrasts are perhaps more than most observers can be expected to comprehend and understand. It is more than we who live here can always understand. But I know that the paradoxes are often explainable and that the polarities are attracted to common values in the center. The value of independence, and all of the variations on that theme, lead to some of the paradoxes. We have all wanted to do what we wanted to do, as long as it did not immediately encroach on those for whom we cared, and we have been reluctant to interfere with others unless there was persistent and vexing irritation. Then our aloof politeness might change in an instant to violent reprisal, often with little discussion. Because we think that we mind our own business and are careful of the rights of others, we don't understand why others aren't perfectly aware of their transgressions. It does not occur to us that the other party might be oblivious to the fact that he is causing a problem, and therefore, we do not trouble ourselves to tell him. We assume that what he does is deliberate and perhaps vindictive. After stewing in our anger and resentment for a time, we act. If we are inclined toward a systematic means of seeking justice, we 'law' the scoundrel. If not, we may take things into our own hands. Violence is usually not random in the mountains. One Harlan, Kentucky surgeon, nettled at what someone had said or written to the effect that he would be afraid to travel in Eastern Kentucky, wrote a letter to a newspaper stating that of all the gunshot victims he had treated, each knew exactly who had shot him and why. The implication is that the violence is personal, growing out of close relationships. It usually involves pride, honor or obligation toward that which is expected of each person. Perhaps at some point the people, who are usually self-effacing and modest, must defend their self-worth. If one holds modesty at a premium, then he expects others to respect and honor that which he is reluctant to talk about—his basic worth. When they do not respect him and his values, he at times reacts violently.

The intense pride in one's place, such as my Uncle Weimer held, together with the pervasive absentee ownership of coal and timber land, tourist traps and summer homes creates an obvious contradiction. But here again, the sense of individualism and privacy, leaving room for the other fellow to pursue his own individual aims while shielded by the same kind of privacy, has been our undoing. While we were defending our own solitude and individualistic goals, we allowed great areas around us to be bought up by strangers. It is true that in the case of mineral rights, we probably thought we were bilking those who were more shrewdly bilking us. This situation has left many of us presiding over the debris from strip mines or living on our ancestral lands among strangers.

The contrasts between the old and the new are everywhere present. Farmers plow tobacco with mules not far from jetports and chemical plants. Old Regular Baptist frame churches sit up the hollow from impressive buildings of mainline denominations. Plaintive folk songs, styled to Bluegrass, are played over the new FM stations along with the beat of rock and the croon of pop. Coal miners who drive Cadillacs also keep fox hounds and play the banjo. Young folks rent evening attire for the Junior-Senior Prom and go home to coal stoves and soup beans. Sensing this attachment to the old ways, alternative life-stylers from upper and middle class backgrounds move in, determined to go back even further in time, but with Rototillers, stereos and an occasional check from anxious parents.

And what does all of this mean? Partially, it is that Appalachians and a great many other Americans are pulled by an ox-mule team of conflicting values—that of reverence for tradition as well as enchantment with the progressive and new. Most mountain people have not hesitated long when new opportunities presented themselves, if they brought more money for the new values which they had developed, having to do with education, health care, a few comforts and more aesthetic opportunities. Working in the mines or factory may have seemed better than trying to raise corn on a hillside, carrying slabs at a sawmill twenty miles from home or digging the dwindling supply of ginseng and other herbs. Yet, there is the worrisome fear that perhaps we have given up more than we gained. It comes through to us that everything is a trade and that there are no free lunches. When one accepts a new way of spending his time, he must give up the old pastimes. Likewise when one accepts someone else's values, he loosens his hold on his old values. St. Paul had admonished the faithful to "hold fast to your traditions, whether by word or epistle." We allow that he was not talking just about religion. Therefore, those of us who can, get that job and the money that goes with it, buy a color TV, freezer, stereo, good vehicle but maybe also a real good banjo, fox hound or rifle, and we try to hold on to a piece of land or buy some that the Florida crowd missed, keep up with the Old Regular Baptists or Pentecostals and listen to country music.

In spite of the despoliation, the imperial pressures from the media, the romantic fakery that one observes on every hand, much that is good is happening in the region. Many are becoming more aware of their heritage and what it means to them. They feel better about themselves. There are more opportunities to make a decent living and to purchase better chances at education, health care, entertainment and artistic development. Some of the younger politicians are more honest than the old. The people make better choices.

But we are still trading our real treasures—values, religion, songs, land, essence—for new and untried things, without knowing that what we lose may be irreplaceable. It behooves us to make shrewd trades, like our horse trading forebears. Else we shall awake one day to find that what our fathers and mothers cherished is but a memory or a fading image on old photographs.

Robert Cooper / Boys on Courthouse Lawn, Glenville

Robert Cooper / Pearl's Bedroom, Auburn

Robert Cooper / *Fields & Pearl Tharpe, Auburn*

Robert Cooper / Bathroom at My Great-grandfather's House, Auburn

Robert Cooper / Elk Street, Gassaway

Robert Cooper / Front Porch at Ruth Ireland's, Auburn

Robert Cooper / Mamie Kennedy, Glenville

Robert Cooper / Riley Murphy, Glenville

Robert Cooper / Lockard Farm, between Cox's Mill & Glenville

Robert Cooper / Mary McMorrow Brown, Stout's Mill

Robert Cooper / Baptist Church, Main Street, Glenville

Robert Cooper / Frozen, Calhoun County

RENA CORNETT

Rena Cornett has always lived within five miles of her birthplace in Eastern Kentucky. She and her husband, Oliver Meade, had eight children and raised as many more from other families. Their home was a gathering place for adults and children alike. Now the children have grown, married, and have children of their own. Oliver and Rena lived alone in their house on the top of Pine Mountain, until Oliver died in October, 1977. Now Rena stays there by herself, but her grandchildren come to visit with her as often as they can.

I was born right near the mouth of Ingram's Creek, October the third in Nineteen and Nineteen. I spent most of my childhood daydreaming. I must have been eight or nine when I started school. I know I never got to go as much as I would like to have.

I was seventeen when I had my first boyfriend, and I never will forget it. A lot of girls ran away and got married, but I never did do that. When I married, it was like an everyday event. I was nineteen, and I just got married and moved out of the house, but I was back everyday or so. But then after my son, Charles, was born, we separated. Just quit.

Shortly after Charles started walking, I married Oliver. He was a good man. I used to bookkeep and cook where he worked. I couldn't tell you what I felt about marrying him. He was a lot older than I, and I gradually grew to love him. A lot of things can happen in forty years, but it seems like yesterday. If I had to do it over again, I'd do it the same way.

I don't think anyone had a better childhood than I did. We were poor, but we were together and we loved each other. That's the way I tried to raise my children. I didn't have the money to dress them, but I always made them wash before dark and then go to bed. I thought it would be dreadful for a child to die dirty, but I do love to see them get dirty. I think they're enjoying life right then.

I think you've got to give a tree or a child room to grow. You need to give everything liberty.

Wendy Ewald

I believe that great-grandparents are the roots of our souls. We're their offspring, and I think that once we learn to love them, we can reach out and touch them.

I learned from my great-grandparents that it takes determination and courage and a will power to face a wilderness life. And I think, if the world turned around today, and I met my great-great-grandparents, from what I found out from my Daddy and Grandpa about them, I could just pick up and walk with them.

Many times when I was young and walked to school alone, I felt my great-grandmother was with me. She would tell me what the name of this flower was and the name of that flower was. I told her yonder in that picture this morning that I'm so sick. I'm not worth a button. She seemed to say to me to get up and try to go on, so I did.

It's good to study anybody. My grandchildren, sometimes they astonish me. I can picture things in them that their parents can't see at all.

I wish parents now would sit down and tell their children where to find the bee tree, how to find the walnut tree that will bear, how to find the mulberry tree, and where to find the slippery elm tree. It would be so much better than criticizing people.

Wendy Ewald

Wendy Ewald

Wendy Ewald

Wendy Ewald

It's somewhat lonely not to have the children around, but I keep myself occupied. I think as Oliver and I grew older, we grew closer together. We had more time with each other, and we had more to talk about.

I think at meal time we each missed our children. I never eat without thinking of the time when eighteen sat down at the table. But then when we were alone, we could take our time and talk as we liked and stay calm as we liked.

I think the older we got, the more we needed each other, and there's nothing better than companionship with an older person.

Oliver was a logger man most of his life, and he loved the trees. Even after he was blind, he went into the woods with other people, and he would feel the trees and try to tell what kind they were.

He built things all the time and when he wasn't working, he was talking. Whatever he did, he enjoyed. He loved the mountains. He didn't want to go anyplace. He just wanted he and I together.

Wendy Ewald

Wendy Ewald

Wendy Ewald

In some ways I'm getting used to Oliver's death and in ways I'm expecting him to come back. I feel like it's my responsibility to carry on from here, and I hope now that Oliver's gone my life can be healthier. I took care of him for eight years, and when he died I was exhausted. I would like to get strong enough to do the work I'd like to do.

I'd like my house to grow old and go down as I do. I'd like it to walk on a cane a while and say, 'Well done. I was made with love and I'm passing with love.'

Wendy Ewald

Earl Dotter

Earl Dotter

Earl Dotter / Setting Temporary Roof Supports

Earl Dotter

Earl Dotter

Earl Dotter

Earl Dotter / Buffalo Creek, West Virginia

Earl Dotter / Black Lung Victim, Mingo, West Virginia

Earl Dotter / Black Lung Victim with His Family

Earl Dotter / Scotia Mine Disaster, Letcher County, Kentucky

Earl Dotter / Scotia Mine Disaster

Earl Dotter / Miner, Buffalo Creek, West Virginia

CATFISH

C. F. 'Catfish' Gray is an herb doctor. His sassafras, slippery elm, and special mixture of 'bitters' bring many people to his two-room house. But more than the herbs, they are attracted by the man.

Catfish is a local person, grounded through years of intimate contact with the earth and its rhythms. He has spent his life in two general areas that are one hundred and ten miles apart and several miles into the hills from rural sections of the Ohio River Valley. Raised in a family of twelve, Catfish was the oldest child. He had ten children of his own. Today he lives alone, separated from his wife of thirty years, but renewed by his daily association with customers, neighbors, and his three sons who live nearby.

Following his fast pace, it is difficult to keep up with him. But what a trail he leads as he weaves his experience into tales of strength and power.

I am Catfish, Man of the Woods, known as a fifth generation herb doctor, and I sell herbs to cure people from all over the Earth, and anybody is welcome to come to my place to visit me.

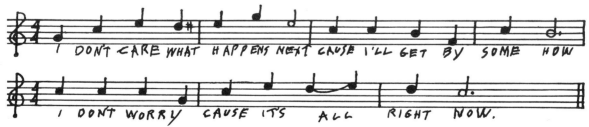

Will Endres

CATFISH MAN OF THE "1967 WOODS

CLARENCE FREDRIC GRAY
ADDRESS = C.F. GRAY
GLEN WOOD. Z. 25520
W.VA. R.I.

NICK NAMES I HAVE HAD.
67 " " NATION WIDE " " EL DURRICO. TO 1936 SASSAFRACE-
-KING = 1942 CATFISH = 1967 NAMED
CAT.FISH.MAN.OF THE WOODS BY-
- CONNIE JO JUSTICE OF THE HUNTINGTON PUBLISH-
-ING COMPANY AND WENT WORLD WIDE. = OLD CITY MARKET
1971 CATFISHES SUPER MARKET 3. AVE. 7.ST. WENT NATION WIDE.
BY DAVE PEYTON

THIS CHART WAS
MADE IN 1971 ON 3RD AVE.
HUNTINGTON W.VA. TIME
TURN THIS READ OTHER SIDE IF YOU HAVE

CATFISH WAS BORN IN A DIVIDED
CHICKEN COOP 10. BY 14. ½ & of the COOP. I WAS BORN
ON THE JACKSON AND ROAN COUNTY LINE. I HAVE Sept 9, 1917
A BIRTH CERTIFIC FROM EACH COUNTY. MAY BE
THE ONLY CASE IN THE WORLD LIKE THAT, I HAVE 5
SISTERS 3 BROTHERS. I STARTED TO SCHOOL AT 8. YRS
OF AGE. AT AGE 18 YRS OLD I FAILED THE SECOND YEAR IN THE FOURTH GRADE WITH 14 Fs AND THE TEACHER TOLD
ME IT WOULD BE. AS WELL FOR ME TO QUIT SCHOOL FOR I COULDNT LEARN ANYTHING ANY WAY SO. I. QUIT.
NEXT THING I DID WENT TO WORK ON A FARM FOR 2 YEARS AND READ THE BIBLE CLEAR THRU. THEN BCAME A
SALESMAN FOR ZANOL PRODUCTS CO AND STARKS FRUIT. CO. AND HELPED BUILD A DUPONT PLANT. WENT THRU THE
PERDUCTION LINES AS A PERFECT FIRST CLASS WORKER. TOOK 17 EXAMS FOR WORLD. 2. FAILED THEM ALL. GOT
MARRIED HAD A WIFE AND 10 CHILDREN 6 GIRLS 4 BOYS THEY WERE ALL AS PRETTY AS COULD BEE LOOKED LIKE ME.
HELPED BUILD 1 PITTSBURG PLATE GLASS CO PLANT. AND LAND SCAPED 15 YEARS. PAINTING. TREE TRIMING WELL I DID
A LITTLE BIT OF EVERY THING UNDER THE SUN. FARMED FOR 13 YEARS ON MY OWN FARM-HELPED TARE DOWN AND REBUILD
I HAD 14 HEART ATACTS IN FIVE 4 YEARS AND CURED MY SELF IN 5 MONTHS AFTER THE DOCTORS GAVE ME UP TO DIE.
THE 26 of AND I AVE TOBACCO WARE HOUSE WORKED MORE HOURS THEN ANY OF THE MEN. = WORKED AT CERMUCIL OPT RTAL
IN GUYAN DOT. GOT BOTH ARMS CAUGHT IN A EIVATOR HAD 2 RUPTURES STILL HAVE ONE. I HAD IN MY LIFE THEIS
DIFFERENT AILMENTS = HEART TROUBLE 14 HEART ATACTS IN 4 YEARS STARTING 1st+ ULSERS HIM ROYDS BROKEN. ARM BLIND EYE DEAF EAR CORNS ON MY TOES HOOPING COUGH
RED MEASELS LITTLE MEASELS CHICKEN POCKS RHOMATIS RHUMATIC FEAVER TONSILLITIS ASMA ARTURITIS BURCITIS. LOW-
-BLOOD PRESSUR HIGH BLOOD PRUSHER TURNED ANCLE INFINTAGO HIP THREW OUT. OF SOCKET 2 TIMES MANY MORE THINGS TO NOMEROS
TO MENTION. 1946 1967 MAY THE FIRST I WAS IN BAD SHAPE BUT WENT TO COLECTING ROOTS HERBS BARK AND,
BERRIES FROM THE FOREST AND SELLING THEM FOR A LIVING FEEDING 12 MOUTHS WITH 9 CHILDREN IN SCHOOL.
NOW I LECTURE AT MARSHAL COLLEGE. AND HIGH SCHOOL. GRADED SCHOOL. LION CLUBS. GARDEN CLUBS. WOMEN CLUBS
BUTY COLLEGES HEALTH FOOD MEETINGS CHURCHES. KINDER GARDENS. GO ON TURES AS A LEAPER. HAD VICE PRESIDENT FROM THE CAPITOL TO SELL
I WAS TAPED AND WITH MOVIES 3 HRS FROM EUROPE. AND STATE OF WASHINGTON. AND CLEVELAND OHIO. HAD A FREE TICKET TO EUROPE FOR 2 WEEK TURE AND A LEADER. I TEACH HORSCOPE. PLANTING SIGNS. WELL
I HAVE BEEN ON TV SEVERAL TIMES I HAVE DELVERED 3 BABBYS. I TEACH PEOPLE HOW THEY CAN GET A BOY
AND UNICE KENEDY. SHRIVER AND HER HUSBAND. 2 GUARDS = HAD WITH BLUE Z& MANY COLLGE PROFESSERS COME TO ME TO LEARN THEIS DIFFRENT KINDS OF HERBS. I DONT KNOW HOW MANY PAPERS AND S MAGIZINES I HAVE BEEN IN. A BIG NUMBER
ASK ME ANY QUESTIONS YOU WILL. AND GET SOME KIND OF AN ANSWER. I TEACH HOW TO HAVE
BABY OR A GIRL BABY IN 10 YEARS FROM NOW AND HAVE IT IN A SIGN TO MATCH THEM SO IT WILL MIND THEM. I TEACH HOW TO HAVE
INTER CORSES BY NATURES PROTECTION AND NOT BCOME PRAGNENT. I TEACH SEX IN A CLEAN AND UNBARRISABLE WAY.
I GO TO CHURCH TWIST A DAY ON SUNDAY AND AS OFTEN AS POSSIBLE OTHER TIMES. ASK ME ANY BIBLE
QUESTONS. THAT IS WHAT I AM HERE FOR. I DO NOT SELL ANY KIND OF DOPE. LIQUOR OR WINE OR TOBACCO
OR MARY WANNA. OR HARRAN OR OPIOM. OR ANY DANGEROUS PLANT. NIGHTSHADE POISON IVY POISON OAK. BLUE COOCH.
OR POISON HIMLOCK.

IF NO EMERGENCYS

I WILL BE OPEN WEDs-THUs FRDs FROM 10 A.M. TO 6 P.M. EVENINGS

READ PHIL. 3:14

WHEN I GET IN FROM THE MOUNTAINS THERE WILL BE A ADD IN SPECIAL ADDS SAYING CATFISH IS BACK FROM THE MOUNTIANS WITH HIS WILD FLOWERS AND GOSTY THINGS

I WILL BE OPEN OTHER DAYS SOME TIMES TOO

FEEL FREE TO ASK ME ANY QUESTIONS I MAY HAVE YOU A GOOD ANSWER. IF I CANT ANSWER YOU
DONT ASK ANY ONE ELS FOR THEY CANT ANSWER IT EITHER. DONT BE BACKWARD OR BASHFUL.

I HAVE FROM 4 to 6 to 900 DIFFRENT ARTICTEES

FOR YOU TO LOOK AT AND BUY. I WILL HAVE DIFFRENT THINGS FROM
TIME TO TIME YOU WILL BE AMAISED. TELL YOUR FRIENDS AND NEIGHBORS AND
ENEMYS THEY MAY LIKE A LITTLE. OF THIS TOO. CATFISH MAN OF THE WOODS

Will Endres / Finding Wild Ginseng

Some of these days your eyes will jump to ginseng like magnets jump to steel.

Will Endres / Gathering Sweet Everlasting

I prayed for God to give me all the knowledge it takes to teach all the people everything about herbs that can be taught. Don't think anything about me. It is God who makes me know what to do.

You can feel the love when you're touching somebody.

In the Spring of 1976, Catfish was asked by the Smithsonian Institution if he would be interested in attending their large American Folklife Festival in Washington, D.C.

Catfish: I know it's a big place.

Smithsonian: You'd talk to a million people a day.

Catfish: Daggone it. I can talk to all I want to here. Just forget about it.

Smithsonian: Yeah, but three thousand dollars?

Catfish: Three thousand dollars ain't a drop in the bucket. You fellars would make ten million dollars off me if I just talked for three weeks.

Smithsonian: You don't want us to make money?

Catfish: That is not the thing at all. I want people to get well, and I may as well be here doctorin' people as be out there talkin' to a big bunch of windjammers who ain't going to do anything but make beer parties and card parties out of it.

Smithsonian: You don't think much of people, do you?

Catfish: I think much of people, but I don't think much of the daggone kind of ways some people does like.

Smithsonian: Don't you like card parties?

Catfish: No!

Smithsonian: Don't you like beer parties?

Catfish: Piddle on it! That's for somebody else to do. That's not for me. I'm not interested!

Smithsonian: You wouldn't play cards with us? You wouldn't drink beer with us?

Catfish: Sure wouldn't!

Smithsonian: What kinda fella are you?

Catfish: I'm just not like you are.

God's got power through spirit that can reach every person, every tree and animal, and everything there is on Earth. He can reach it with his power, and make it do what he wants.

I'm sixty-one years old, and feel best I've ever felt in my life, and I bet you I've danced a thousand jigs in a month last summer.

Lyn Adams / Pig Pen in January

Lyn Adams / Bird Rock

Lyn Adams

Lyn Adams

Lyn Adams / Homecoming

Lyn Adams / Widow Combs

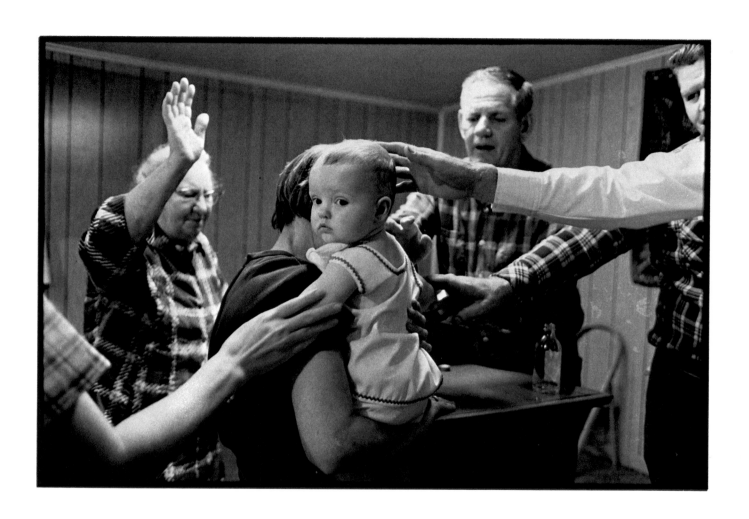

Lyn Adams / Ceremony: Lloyd Collins Church

TWO FAMILIES

THE CAUDILL FAMILY

Arlie and Crow, Brothers
Brice, 24, Nephew
Melissa, 9, Niece

THE CHILDERS FAMILY

Hettie and Burley, Parents
Children: Homer, 27
            Jamie, 26
            Celina, 19
            Roy, 18
            Corrine, 17
            Junior, 12
            Freddie, 9

Shelby Adams / Brice, Spring 1974

Shelby Adams / Melissa & Brice, Spring 1978

Shelby Adams / Arlie, Summer 1975

Shelby Adams / Crow, Summer 1975

Shelby Adams / Christmas Day 1976

Shelby Adams / Self-portrait with Arlie, Winter 1977

Shelby Adams / Arlie, Summer 1977

Shelby Adams / Hettie, Celina, & Homer, Fall 1977

Shelby Adams / Celina, Christmas, 1977

Shelby Adams / Freddie & Celina, Summer 1976

Shelby Adams / Hettie & Burley, Winter 1977

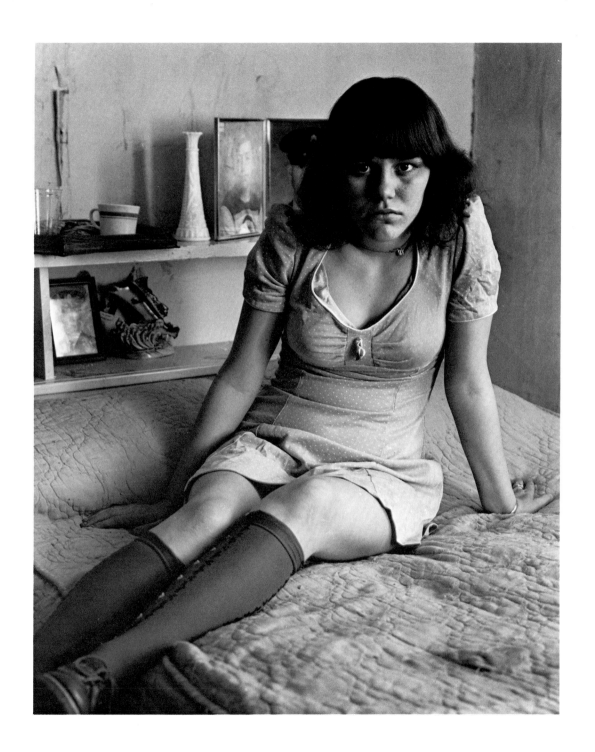

Shelby Adams / *Corrine, Winter* 1977

Linda Mansberger / *My Cousins, Sherry & Jimmy*

Linda Mansberger / My Nephew, Jamie

Linda Mansberger / *Neighbor & Dog*

Linda Mansberger / My Friend Tommy, the Motorcrosser

Linda Mansberger / My Brother, Randy

Linda Mansberger / My Brother-in-law, Mike

Linda Mansberger / The Archers: My Brother Roger, Mike, & Neighbors

THE AUTHORS

ROBERT COLES, a child psychologist on the staff of the Harvard University Health Services, is the author of many books in the fields of psychology, sociology, and literature. Coles spent time in Appalachia over several years, visiting and interviewing families for Volume Two of his *Children of Crisis* series, subtitled *Migrants, Sharecroppers, and Mountaineers*. Coles also has had an interest in photography for many years, has written texts for many photography books, and is a Contributing Editor for *Aperture* magazine.

LOYAL JONES was born in 1928 in North Carolina and grew up on a mountain farm in Clay County. He has written numerous articles on Appalachia and two studies, on singers Bradley Kincaid and Bascom Lamar Lunsford, are awaiting publication. He is presently Director of the Appalachian Center at Berea College in Kentucky.

THE PHOTOGRAPHERS

LYN ADAMS moved to Perry County, Kentucky in 1974. Her interest lies in photographing the people of Appalachia as they move through the daily business of life, in discovering the drama of the undramatic and the commonplace. She relates the Appalachian people to the 'general flux of humanity,' focusing on commonalities rather than differences.

SHELBY ADAMS was born and raised in Letcher County, Kentucky. In 1968, he left to go to art school. He now lives in Cincinnati, but makes frequent trips back to visit his family and the two families he has photographed. He has taken pictures of the Caudill family for four years and the Childers family for two years. He works with a 4×5 view camera and uses Polaroid film to let his subjects share in the excitement of making the images.

ROBERT COOPER began to photograph the area around his hometown, Sutton, West Virginia in 1966. In a way he photographs his autobiography by his evolving relation with his hometown and the surrounding area. He has worked on a photographic essay of Central West Virginia for several years and continues to work there now as a photographer-in-residence for the Arts and Humanities Council in Braxton County.

EARL DOTTER's major work as a photographer in Appalachia has primarily focused on coal miners and their communities. From 1973 to 1977 he was the photographer for the *United Mine Workers Journal*. His work focuses on the workplace, health and safety of Appalachian coal mines.

WILL ENDRES is a native of Charleston, West Virginia. In the summer of 1975 he began studying with and photographing 'Catfish' Gray, an herb doctor living near Glenwood, West Virginia. Through photographs and tape recordings, he captures the spontaneity and energy of this man. Will earns his living gathering and selling herbs in much the same way as Catfish.

WENDY EWALD moved to Letcher County, Kentucky in 1975. Soon after, she began photographing Rena Meade, who lives in Cowan, a neighboring community. Wendy portrays Rena's life, her relationships with the land and her family, and her passage through life's most difficult transition—the death of her husband of 40 years.

LINDA MANSBERGER has always lived in Morgantown, West Virginia. Following in the tradition of her grandfather, also a photographer, she has documented her own working-class family whose life style and values are typical of many Appalachian people. She has recorded their daily life and captured their strength and ingenuity in coping with whatever comes along.

The Mountain Photography Workshop is a group of seven photographers working in Kentucky and West Virginia. In July, 1976 we were awarded a National Endowment for the Arts grant to document the Appalachian regions of Kentucky and West Virginia. We were all photographing on our own in the mountains, so this gave us a chance to meet and work with other photographers who were also concerned with Appalachia.

Each photographer chose one subject to document. We met every two months to talk about the work we had done. At the end of a year, as a group we began to edit the photographs and decide how best they could be used. We felt it was more important for each of us to look in depth at an aspect of the culture we were most concerned with rather than to document the region overall. This book is the result of our work together for a year and a half. It is a personal view of a people and a landscape, which has nurtured us as photographers and individuals.

WENDY EWALD